C000126736

1,000,000 Books

are available to read at

www.ForgottenBooks.com

Read online
Download PDF
Purchase in print

ISBN 978-1-397-26077-2
PIBN 11372073

This book is a reproduction of an important historical work. Forgotten Books uses state-of-the-art technology to digitally reconstruct the work, preserving the original format whilst repairing imperfections present in the aged copy. In rare cases, an imperfection in the original, such as a blemish or missing page, may be replicated in our edition. We do, however, repair the vast majority of imperfections successfully; any imperfections that remain are intentionally left to preserve the state of such historical works.

Forgotten Books is a registered trademark of FB &c Ltd.
Copyright © 2018 FB &c Ltd.
FB &c Ltd, Dalton House, 60 Windsor Avenue, London, SW19 2RR.
Company number 08720141. Registered in England and Wales.

For support please visit www.forgottenbooks.com

1 MONTH OF
FREE
READING

at

www.ForgottenBooks.com

By purchasing this book you are eligible for one month membership to ForgottenBooks.com, giving you unlimited access to our entire collection of over 1,000,000 titles via our web site and mobile apps.

To claim your free month visit: www.forgottenbooks.com/free1372073

* Offer is valid for 45 days from date of purchase. Terms and conditions apply.

English
Français
Deutsche
Italiano
Español
Português

www.forgottenbooks.com

Mythology Photography **Fiction**
Fishing Christianity **Art** Cooking
Essays Buddhism Freemasonry
Medicine **Biology** Music **Ancient
Egypt** Evolution Carpentry Physics
Dance Geology **Mathematics** Fitness
Shakespeare **Folklore** Yoga Marketing
Confidence Immortality Biographies
Poetry **Psychology** Witchcraft
Electronics Chemistry History **Law**
Accounting **Philosophy** Anthropology
Alchemy Drama Quantum Mechanics
Atheism Sexual Health **Ancient History**
Entrepreneurship Languages Sport
Paleontology Needlework Islam
Metaphysics Investment Archaeology
Parenting Statistics Criminology
Motivational

HARRY B. THAYER

TWELVE YEARS

OF THE

TELEPHONE PIONEERS

OF AMERICA

Presented to the
Telephone Pioneers of America
at the
Tenth Annual Banquet
by The American Telephone
and Telegraph Company·

ATLANTIC CITY, N. J.
October 20, 1923

A Great Brotherhood

❦

"Fellow Pioneers:—I greet you as a great brotherhood, interdependent, in that each of you have assisted and been assisted by the other; intercommunity, in that throughout this whole organization is only one common thought, resulting in one common policy, which has actuated one common movement; universal, in that the genius which originated the policy, and the purposes, and the enthusiasm which has carried it out so wonderfully is the great Bell System, and will be the great system of the future, be it private corporation, or government-owned, bound-less and without limitations other than those of geographic, national and commercial nature."

Theo. a. Vail

Third Annual Convention
Telephone Pioneers of America
Chicago, Illinois
October 17, 1913

CHRONOLOGY
OF THE
TELEPHONE PIONEERS OF AMERICA

October 1, 1910
First membership paper circulated by Henry W. Pope.

August 21, 1911
Call for first meeting issued.

November 1 and 2, 1911
First annual meeting in Boston. Theodore N. Vail elected President; Constitution and By-Laws adopted.

February 9, 1912
Alexander Graham Bell elected first honorary member by Board of Directors.

November 14 and 15, 1912
Second annual meeting in New York City. Mr. Vail re-elected.

October 17 and 18, 1913
Third annual meeting in Chicago. Distinction between "Pioneers" and "Junior Pioneers" abolished. Mr. Vail re-elected.

October 29 and 30, 1914
Fourth annual meeting in Richmond. Mr. Vail re-elected.

September 21 and 22, 1915
Fifth annual meeting in San Francisco. Mr. Vail re-elected.

October 27 and 28, 1916
Sixth annual meeting in Atlanta. Mr. Vail re-elected.

September 10 and 11, 1920
Seventh annual meeting in Montreal, no meetings having been held in 1917, 1918 or 1919 because of the war. Harry B. Thayer elected President.

October 25 and 26, 1921
Eighth annual meeting in St. Louis. Organization of local chapters and a General Assembly provided for; term of President limited to one year. John J. Carty elected President.

September 29 and 30, 1922
Ninth annual meeting, and First meeting of the General Assembly at Cleveland. Leonard H. Kinnard elected President.

Twelve Years of the Telephone Pioneers

By WILLIAM CHAUNCY LANGDON

THE organization of the Telephone Pioneers of America began in comradeship—the comradeship of achievement together. Alexander Graham Bell was the last of the great individual inventors. Working alone, he thought out the theory of the electric transmission of speech, discovered how to use the undulatory current, and invented the telephone. But the development of the telephone—as an instrument, as a communication system, as a business organization and public utility—has been the result of teamwork. The membership of the Telephone Pioneers of America is made up of those who through a notable number of years have contributed to that development. In the spirit of comradeship they did their work; and the spirit of comradeship brought them together into this fellowship.

When the Telephone Pioneers was started, in 1911, the requirements for membership restricted the privilege to those who had worked in the early days, and emphasized the contributions of those who were in the business before the year 1891. But even in 1911 there was clear realization that pioneers are not only those who are the first to begin a new advance, but that as problems, numerous and often apparently insoluble, always bar the way, the true pioneer is he who goes ahead with faith, intelligence and enthusiasm, now as well as then, and fifty years hence as well as now.

So, in these twelve years the Pioneer spirit, stimulated by reminiscence of the past, has shaped the organization up for vital service in the present. It has rallied to its standard the younger generations of Telephone men and women, and endowed them with the legacy of a high and fine tradition of continuing comradeship.

The Telephone Pioneers was started by three men—Henry W. Pope, Charles R. Truex, and Thomas B. Doolittle. The idea originated with Mr. Pope. In 1880 he organized the National Telephone Exchange Association, the first series of conferences in the telephone industry. He therefore naturally appreciated the value of such organizations. Mr. Pope talked the idea of an association of telephone pioneers over with Mr. Truex, and then together they took up the question with Mr. Doolittle. The three decided to find out how such an organization would be received. Their first step was to consult Mr. Vail. He heartily approved of the plan and gave them from the start his cordial support. Accordingly they constituted themselves an Organizing Committee.

The Committee drafted a membership paper, and took it personally to all the

HENRY W. POPE, *Secretary*
1911-1914

prominent early telephone men they could reach, asking them to sign it and give their support to the plan. The date of this paper was October 1, 1910. It read as follows:

THE TELEPHONE PIONEERS
of ·
AMERICA

It has seemed advisable to a number of the pioneers of the Telephone industry to form an Association, to embrace, to such extent as may be found practicable, the early workers in the telephone field, under the proposed caption of

"THE TELEPHONE PIONEERS OF AMERICA"

for the purpose of renewing and perpetuating friendships, and fostering and encouraging such other worthy and appropriate purposes as may from time to time be suggested and approved.

You are cordially invited and requested to indicate, by the affixing of your signature hereto, your willingness to join in the formation of such proposed Association.

(Signed) HENRY W. POPE.

Space was provided for the signatures, addresses, dates of entering the telephone service, present occupations, and titles of those who promised to join the organization.

The first names signed were

Henry W. Pope	Thomas D. Lockwood	C. E. Scribner
Thos. B. Doolittle	Chas. A. Nicholson	Enos M. Barton
Charles R. Truex	Alfred E. Holcomb	Edward J. Hall
Wm. Dunlap Sargent	Bernard E. Sunny	F. A. Pickernell
Frank B. Knight	Angus S. Hibbard	Chas. H. Wilson
John H. Cahill	Theo. N. Vail	H. B. Thayer
George W. Foster	J. J. Carty	C. F. Sise

On the two copies of this first paper now in the archives
of the Telephone Pioneers there are 169 signatures. These
may be considered to comprise the first membership of the
association.

In the spring of 1911 the Committee followed this personal appeal with a letter to all the more distant early telephone men whose addresses they could obtain. This letter
read as follows:

15 Dey Street, New York, N. Y.

March 1, 1911.

Mr. Geo. C. Maynard,
Dear Sir:

There is in process of formation an organization with the tentative
title of "The Telephone Pioneers of America" for the purpose of renewing and perpetuating friendships and encouraging such other worthy
and appropriate purposes as may from time to time be suggested and
approved.

The preliminary requirements are: That any person of good standing engaged or employed in the service twenty-five years prior to date
of application and at any time thereafter continuously in the Bell service
for five years is acceptable.

At the present time nearly every important official, meeting these
requirements, has signed, and, should you feel inclined, we shall be
pleased to receive your application.

Yours truly,

(Signed) HENRY W. POPE.

Note: These requirements are only tentative, subject to future amendment or adjustment. H. W. P.

In consequence of this activity it was possible for the
Committee to issue on May 1, 1911, an advanced list of the
membership comprising 235 names. By October 1, 1911,
the number had increased to 439 names.

On August 21, 1911, the call for the first meeting of
the Telephone Pioneers was issued for November 2 and 3,
in Boston. The cooperation of the American Telephone &
Telegraph Company and of the New England Telephone
& Telegraph Company was gladly given and a Boston Committee of Arrangements was appointed by the latter Company with W. J. Denver as Chairman and A. N. Bullens
as Secretary.

THE MEETING IN BOSTON

On the morning of Thursday, November 2, the meeting
was called to order at the Hotel Somerset, Boston, by
Thomas B. Doolittle. 246 Pioneers were in attendance.
General Thomas Sherwin, President of the New England
Telephone & Telegraph Company was chosen Temporary
Chairman, and Henry W. Pope, Temporary Secretary.

In his address of welcome General Sherwin finely stated
the object of the proposed organization.

"The men assembled here have long
been engaged in the active work of organizing and building up the telephone system in
this country, and I know it affords all of us
pleasure to come together for the purpose of
forming and perpetuating this Association, which shall keep alive the traditions of the past, the story of our
experience in doing each on his part
something for the development of this
wonderful art, and the friendly
association formed during our
service in the same field."

*This and other quotations which fol-
low are only given in part. The complete
text may be found in the Proceedings of
the several Annual Meetings.

At the same time he sounded the key-note of the continuing character of all pioneer work.

"The Association, too, cannot but have its value and encouraging influence for those who, in the future, are to carry forward the work which we of this day have begun, enlarging, broadening and perfecting the system and its usefulness, to an extent beyond anything which we can now contemplate."

The meeting then proceeded to the adoption of the Constitution. The name was formally determined as the Telephone Pioneers of America, and the purpose of the organization was defined in Article I.

"The Association is formed for the purpose of recalling and perpetuating the facts, traditions and memories attaching to the early history of the telephone and the telephone system; preserving the names and records of the participants in the establishment and extension of this great system of electrical intercommunication; the promotion, renewal and continuance of the friendships and fellowships made during the progress of the telephone industry between those interested therein; and the encouragement of such other meritorious objects consistent with the foregoing as may be desirable."

In Article II the requirement for membership was reduced to 21 years from the 25 years at first proposed.

"Any person of good standing shall be eligible for membership who at any time prior to twenty-one years of the date of application was engaged in the telephone business or its associated interests, and was at any time thereafter continuously in said service for a period of five years; or any person who in the opinion of the Executive Committee shall have rendered service beneficial to the telephone interests, prior to the year 1891, may be enrolled for membership upon receiving a majority vote of the Executive Committee."

The election of permanent officers under the Constitution resulted in the choice of the following Pioneers for

THEODORE N. VAIL

the first year organization: President, Theodore N. Vail; Vice Presidents, F. H. Bethell, W. T. Gentry, B. E. Sunny, E. B. Field; Executive Committee, Thomas D. Lockwood, J. J. Carty, F. A. Houston.   Thomas B. Doolittle and Charles R. .Truex were appointed to the Committee by the President.

General'Sherwin then yielded the chair to Mr. Gentry, and the meeting proceeded to the adoption of the By-Laws. Beside the usual provisions the By-Laws placed the chief active direction in the hands of the Executive Committee and divided the membership into three classes, Honorary Pioneers, Pioneers, and Junior Pioneers.   A Pioneer was defined as one whose connection with the telephone industry dates prior to the year 1891, and a Junior Pioneer as one who has served twenty-one years subsequent to that time.   The dues were fixed at $5.00 for the first year and $2.00 for every year thereafter.

The first address of the Telephone Pioneer Conventions was delivered by Alexander Graham Bell at the opening of the afternoon session.   The tremendous applause with which he was greeted when, with Mr. Fish and Mr. Lockwood, the other speakers of the afternoon, he was escorted to the platform by Mr. Angus S. Hibbard and Mr. Melville Egleston, attested the enthusiastic cordiality of the members to the Inventor of the Telephone.

Dr. Bell's address dealt with the period of the genesis of the telephone, giving personal reminiscences of the years from 1874 to 1877.   It was most interesting to all the early workers who listened to him, while his modesty with regard to his own achivement in his generous tribute to their development of his invention was gratifying and inspiring.

"I feel it a little presumptuous upon my part to try to speak of the telephone to telephone men. You have all gone so far beyond me! Why, the little telephone system that I look back upon—what is it compared to the mighty system that goes through the whole extent of our country today? It is to you that this great development is due, and I feel that it behooves me to speak very modestly of the little beginning that led to this great end. I cannot tell you anything about the telephone. I cannot speak to you about undulating current, intermittent current and pulsatory current. I belong to the past; you belong to the present."

It showed that he not only appreciated the development of the telephone when he foretold it as a vision of the future in 1878, but that he appreciated it no less in 1911 when he saw that vision realized before him by the men who were listening to him.

The address of Thomas D. Lockwood, the last address of the day, was also of the character of personal remi-niscence. He took up the story at the time that Dr. Bell left off and gave first hand accounts of interesting and important incidents in the early days of the National Bell Telephone Company, from the time when he first heard Dr. Bell lecture on the telephone in Chickering Hall, New York, and the time when Mr. Vail abruptly hired him to work for the telephone Company down through the 80's. Through the two addresses of Dr. Bell and Mr. Lockwood the thread of personal experience ran down through more than ten years of the early days of the telephone.

Frederick P. Fish, President of the American Telephone & Telegraph Company from 1901 to 1907, was the other speaker of this afternoon of notable addresses. He came between the other two addresses. His address was in-spiring. With glowing tributes to Dr. Bell, for "what he did was one of the greatest things in the history of the world" and he was "the only man who lived who had the requisite characteristics, the requisite equipment, to have invented the telephone;" and to Mr. Vail as "the man who was doing the most direct, definite and effective work for the promotion of this enterprise," and as "a leader whom everyone will love and follow, because he has the right kind of cordial regard and respect for every man who works with him," Mr. Fish centered his message upon the future of the telephone and of the pioneer organization.

The forward-looking inspiration of Mr. Fish's address will be recalled by a few brief extracts:

"I think that the one thing in which a man can take the most pleasure in any generation that has existed since the beginning of time is that he has been in close touch with the art of the aspirations of his own day; that he has been absorbed in that kind of work which characterizes the spirit of his time. Everyone of us has had to that extent with which he has been associated with telephone work, the opportunity to participate in one thing that more than any other is typical of the spirit of this day. There can be no question that when the history of our times is written this development of the telephone, with all its consequences, will stand out as the most conspicuous thing that we have accomplished. I understand that the pioneers must be men who were associated with the company prior to a certain date. I am not at all sure but that there will be a new definition of "pioneer" some time, and that you will extend that date, for I think it not at all impossible that even today we are to a certain extent in the beginning of things, so that thirty, forty, or fifty years from now the men of that time will look back at the wonderful work of Mr. Carty, the work of our engineers, commercial men, business men and operating men of today, and will say, 'Wonderful as that was, just see what has happened since! The men of 1911 were really only pioneers!'"

As valuable an element as any in the meeting was the opportunity offered for renewing old friendships and making new. The mingling of the Pioneers at the Convention headquarters, in the dining-rooms, on visits to telephone exchanges, on the automobile trip to Lexington and Concord, and at the banquet with which the meeting closed, accomplished as much as any formal part of the programme. But the working of the spirit of comradeship among people great and enjoyable and important as it is, and though one of the chief purposes for which the organization was formed, is far too elusive to estimate or chronicle.

Thus was the Telephone Pioneers of America started forth on its career of inspiring service.

THE MEETING IN NEW YORK CITY

The Second Annual Convention of the Telephone Pioneers of America met in New York City at the Hotel Astor on Thursday and Friday, November 14 and 15, 1912. The General Committee of Arrangements, representing the American Telephone & Telegraph Company, the New York Telephone Company, the Western Electric Company, and the Telephone Pioneers of America, consisted of H. F. Thurber, H. S. Brooks, A. S. Hibbard, Gerard Swope and H. W. Pope.

The sessions were presided over by F. H. Bethell as Vice President. A re-definition of the term Pioneer was early considered, following the suggestion that Mr. Fish made in

Statue of Liberty.

his address at the Boston meeting in 1911. The general
desire was to abolish the grade of Junior Pioneer. In accordance with the Constitution and By-Laws therefore
formal notice was given that at the next meeting of the
Telephone Pioneers, in 1913, such an amendment would be
brought up for action.

Since the first meeting of the Telephone Pioneers, the
Executive Committee had on February 9, 1912, elected
Alexander Graham Bell the first Honorary Member. At
the New York meeting Thomas D. Lockwood proposed
that Francis Blake be elected an Honorary Member. In
his address Mr. Lockwood outlined Mr. Blake's career in
general and especially his work for the Telephone Company
and his chief contribution in the transmitter which bears
his name. Mr. Blake was unanimously elected by acclama-
tion and the Executive Committee subsequently took the
necessary action to confirm the vote of the meeting.

In the election of officers the same were chosen as had
been elected the previous year. Mr. Vail was elected President of the Telephone Pioneers by a separate vote every
year as long as he lived.

There were six addresses given at the afternoon session.
The first was by Thomas A. Watson. He gave very delightful personal reminiscences of the days of his association with
Dr. Bell, in general covering the same years, 1874 to 1877.
Thus the two addresses together give the two sides of the
story of the invention of the telephone from the stand-
points of the two who were concerned in it. Mr. Bethell
introduced Mr. Watson; Mr. Gentry the others.

The brief address of Emile Berliner was also reminiscent
in character. He told about his theory and use of the prin-

ciple of loose contact in his transmitter. His account of his experiments in this work were both clear and interesting, and added a valuable item to the personal statements of telephone inventors regarding the early days.

Union N. Bethell, one of the second crop of Pioneers, as he called himself, centered his address upon the contemporary state of development of the telephone industry. He gave a quick sketch of the history of communications from the report of the surrender of Cornwallis at Yorktown, in 1781, to the uniting of the telephone and the telegraph by Theodore N. Vail, in 1908, a union which was soon to be dissolved though the cooperation has continued. He told of the solution of the complex commercial problems and the message rate by Edward J. Hall, Jr. He spoke of the financial problems, the legal problems, the problems of the coordination of the manifold phases of the telephone industry, and of general administration. As he drew toward the close of his address, there was a passage, pertinent to the organization of the Telephone Pioneers, which may well with slight omissions be quoted.

"We are now better able than ever before to discuss plans, consider measures and determine from the combined experiences of all what is best for the several branches of the service. Besides obtaining uniformity in practice, there has been provided a more ready means of developing ideas and suggestions for future improvements. Greater than ever before is the opportunity for individual initiative. The time never was and never will be when the stability and the progress of this vast enterprise has depended or will depend on the strength, the energy and the intellectual ability of any individual or small group of individuals. The virility and vigor of the organization as a whole has depended, and will continue to depend, on the virility and vigor existing throughout the mass and permeating all its parts. A great and successful leader among us is he who inspires and encourages, and who rightly uses the spirit which wells up to his hands from the myriads of springs whose sources are found among his loyal followers. Moreover, as has been demonstrated time and time again, especially in recent years, every soldier in this Bell army carries in his knapsack a marshal's baton.

"Some of us find comfort in looking to the years that are behind us, while others find their chief delight in looking to the future. I congratulate you all—to those looking to the past because of the high and honorable nature of the work with which you have been identified—to those looking to the future because of what lies before you in its future development. The character of the work you know full well. The transmission of intelligence by electricity is an active and effective agent in the advancement of civilization throughout the world."

Samuel G. McMeen in his short address stressed the same point. Speaking of the great expansion of telephone development in the future, he said:

"Many of us were attracted to the art because it was interesting as a scientific subject. Its scientific side long has been dwarfed by its great social and commercial features. I, for one, long felt it a great thing, but never felt how very great a thing it was until last year in Boston. That first Pioneers' meeting was one of the memorable events of history. Let us look back on what has been done with wonder and with pride; let us be grateful for having lived in this period of marvels. But let us not forget to be duly modest in the face of the great things that are yet to be."

John J. Carty, who also spoke but briefly, suggested for consideration in these meetings of the Telephone Pioneers the work that was done in one of the formative periods of telephone development, the years from 1886 to 1890, such as the work done by the Switchboard Conferences on the metallic circuit switchboard and the underground cable, or the episodes of the great Cortlandt Street switchboard, which was obsolete before it could be put in use, so rapid was the sweep of development, and the work on the first comprehensive specification for a central station, the Thirty-Eighth Street Exchange in New York. He emphasized the value of such personal reminiscences as the addresses of Dr. Bell, Mr. Watson, Mr. Berliner, and Mr. Lockwood, and urged that gathering such valuable first-hand statements as material, a definite, if not formal, historical direction be given to the interests of the association. Reading the purposes of the organization as set forth in the Constitution and giving concrete instances, he said:

"I have been thinking of the origin of our Society and of its wonderful future. What is the best way to perpetuate it and what is the most wholesome and healthy form of growth for our institution to take? Every man here is capable of contributing important historical data in the form of documents, recollections, apparatus, photographs, etc. I suggest therefore, gentlemen, that between now and the next meeting, the direction in which our growth shall take place, the functions we shall perform, be very carefully considered, and that we give careful thought to the question whether or not we should not, in fact if not in name, be the Telephone Pioneers of America and the American Telephone Historical Society."

This suggestion, the Proceedings of subsequent years show, received careful and continuous consideration.

The session closed with a very gracious speech from a visiting telephone man from England, whom Mr. Gentry asked Mr. Lockwood, as a personal friend, to introduce. This was J. E. Kingsbury of London, the author of the well-known work, "The Telephone and Telephone Exchanges." Mr. Kingsbury spoke very appreciatively of his pleasure in being present at the meeting, told some interesting incidents of personal experience in the early days of the telephone in England, and cordially endorsed what Mr. Carty had said concerning the historical responsibilities of such an organization as the Telephone Pioneers.

In the evening of November 14th members of the New York Telephone Society presented an extravaganza on the stage of the grand ballroom of the Hotel Astor for the visiting Pioneers. It was announced as a Cataclysm in One Spasm, entitled Examinations. It was written by Angus S. Hibbard. On the second day of the meeting 499 Pioneers were taken in 110 automobiles up the Hudson River to Briarcliff Lodge. There luncheon was served, and afterwards games and athletic sports attested the virility and prowess of men of the Bell System. In the evening the Convention closed with a banquet at the Astor.

Already the influence of the organization was making itself felt, and was reflected in the press. The special significance of these meetings was noticed by the "Telegraph and Telephone Age."

"One not familiar with the facts might have assumed, as an onlooker, that it was a convention of telephone officials only, rather than officials and subordinate employes together. But in this instance they were neither; all lines of distinction were for the time being obliterated; they were all Pioneers. There are no official distinctions in the membership of the Association—all members are on an equality. Thus it is we find the president, vice presidents, engineers, superintendents, linemen, clerks, etc., all mingling as brothers, bound by the bonds of fellowship in one common cause."

THE MEETING IN CHICAGO

The Chicago meeting of the Telephone Pioneers of America was opened by the President of the organization, Theodore N. Vail, in person. It was cause for great pleasure and gratification that the situation in his affairs and the condition of his health were such that Mr. Vail was able to be present. The date of the Convention had been postponed one day to meet his engagements, and his appearance on the platform at the Congress Hotel on the morning of Friday, October 17, 1913, was greeted with an enthusiastic ovation.

Mr. Vail's opening address was simply one of greeting but it was notable for the concise characterization of the telephone industry and the pioneer organization which is printed at the head of this volume. He then introduced Bernard E. Sunny to welcome the Telephone Pioneers to the City of Chicago.

There was much to Mr. Sunny's address beside the cordial welcome he extended. Speaking for the moment as in a way the representative of the outside public, he depicted the gathering of the telephone clan from out of all sorts of occupations, from telegraphers to physicians, and their training through long experience for standardized cooperation. Of this he said humorously:

"There was so much to be done and so little to do with that almost everyone tried his hand at inventing, and a lack of prior mechanical or electrical experience for such a task, which was the rule rather than the exception, proved no bar. The strength and vitality of Bell's invention were established when it did not succumb to the early inventions of switchboards and other devices, some of them fearfully and wonderfully made, although it must in justice be said that out of the variety of ideas included in the different types of switchboards came the standard multiple switchboard which was generally adopted."

Congress Hotel,
Chicago, Ill.

He then gave an account and paid tribute to the work of the National Telephone Exchange Association (1880–1890) which contributed so materially to the development of the spirit and practice of cooperation and to the leading up through standardization to the great results of the present period.   His whole review he focused on the superior quality of telephone people, both men and women, in the early days and at all times.

"It was the greatest good fortune that the telephone from the beginning was in the hands of men whose confidence in its utility never faltered and who had the courage and patience to meet and overcome every difficulty.   Furthermore, it was the greatest good fortune that these men, strangers to each other in the earlier years, differing in their views and policies with reference to practical questions of service, were alike in the enforcement of the highest business ideals in the conduct of the business at all times and under all conditions.   As a result, no industry enjoys the confidence of the public to a greater degree."

After Mr. Sunny's address, Mr. Vail turned over the chair to the first Vice President, F. H. Bethell   The meeting then proceeded to the transaction of business.   The distinction in the membership between Pioneers and Junior Pioneers was abolished and the selection of the Secretary was delegated to the Executive Committee.   In the election of officers for the ensuing year, at the suggestion of Mr. Lockwood, Mr. Vail was elected President unanimously by a rising vote and the Secretary then cast the required ballot. The officers chosen for the year 1914 were: President, Theodore N. Vail; Vice Presidents, Thomas D. Lockwood, Thomas B. Doolittle, Charles F. Sise, and George E. McFarland; Treasurer, George D. Milne; Executive Committee, Angus S. Hibbard, Charles G. DuBois, Charles E.

Scribner. The members of the Executive Committee appointed by the President were Edgar F. Sherwood and
James T. Moran. Henry W. Pope was reappointed Secretary by the Executive Committee. Mr. Bethell then
yielded the chair to Mr. Lockwood as the new senior
Vice President. Mr. Lockwood was most of the time the
presiding officer for the next four annual meetings.

The business had been disposed of with such good dis-
patch that there was still time before the natural hour for
adjourning. Mr. Lockwood occupied this time with an
extemporaneous address about the development of telegraph exchanges before the invention of the telephone and
of the experimental telephone exchange of Isaac D. Smith,
in Hartford, Connecticut, in 1877.

There were three addresses delivered at the afternoon
session. The first was by Nathan C. Kingsbury. With
the conviction that the work of the Pioneers is by no means
finished, Mr. Kingsbury presented the contemporaneous,
situation in the telephone industry to the pioneers of the
present. He began by calling attention to the vital
problem of securing money for the enormous expenditures
necessary for the extension and operation of the telephone
system, and the rapidity with which extension and improve-
ment of service has grown.

"Only a few years ago it was a cause of great congratulation and a
reason for compliment to the telephone engineers that it was possible
to talk from New York to Philadelphia or to Boston. Today if one cannot secure a good talk from New York to Chicago, it is an occasion for
criticism of the telephone company. The successes of the past call for
greater achievements in the future. The engineers and construction
men are continually busy with problems of transmission; our underground systems are being extended and the intricate engineering and

construction details necessary to make these systems available for commercial use are being worked out as fast as possible. We have assumed the slogan and the responsibility of universal service."

Vivid illustrations illumined his discourse, as when he said:

"Dating from the inception of this government's work on the Panama Canal, the Bell System has spent more money in improving and extending its plant than the government has expended in the digging of the canal."

A large part of his address Mr. Kingsbury devoted to the work of the Public Service Commissions and the relation of the Telephone Company to them as the official representatives of the public. The greatest problem of all, he said, was the giving of service to the public. All other problems were but parts of that great problem.

"Why do we enter into financial arrangements? For no other purpose than to give service. Why do we delve into the secrets of nature in our engineering department and translate these secrets into plain facts for the construction department? For the purpose of giving service. What is the legitimate method of meeting opposition? By giving a superior service. Why do we foster friendly relations with the public? In order that the public may purchase and appreciate our service. Why do we take steps to justify our acts before public officials? Merely that they may understand our problems and our methods of giving service. This problem is more and more difficult of solution. More is required of us at the present time in the way of service than ever before. In almost any other line of endeavor there is an alternative to which people may turn in case their usual reliance fails, but if we should fail there is no possible alternative. Hence our great responsibility. And there is great joy in the solving of these problems. I think we are engaged in the most difficult and at the same time the most interesting business in the world. We become absorbed in the joy of it, for we are performing a high type of civic service, and there is always joy in service."

The second speaker was Thomas B. Doolittle. In his charmingly frank manner and with full personal detail he gave his friends assembled before him in the meeting an autobiographical address. Beginning with his connection with the manufacturing of barbed wire at Bridgeport, Connecticut, in the 60's and early 70's, he told of "The Bridgeport Social Telegraph Association" which he organized; of the fare register and how that brought him into connection with the telephone; of the invention and after many troubles the introduction of hard-drawn copper wire; of his experiences with the switchboard problem; of his conflict as a telephone manager with the Western Union; and his service developing toll lines under President John E. Hudson. It was a delightful contribution both to history and to biography.

The last address of the day was by Thomas A. Watson. His most interesting address at the New York meeting the previous year, 1912, telling the story of the invention of the telephone from his own point of view and throwing such graphic side-lights on the early work and personality of Alexander Graham Bell, only made the Pioneers want to hear more. So Mr. Watson graciously acceded to their desire and gave them the whole story again in more detail. Under the title of "The Birth and Babyhood of the Telephone," this address of Mr. Watson's at the Chicago, 1913, Convention of the Telephone Pioneers has been widely disseminated. It is not necessary therefore to give a résumé of it here. Reprinted in some of the Telephone Company magazines, as a pamphlet, and as a book, many thousands of copies of this address have been issued. The demand for it as a lecture has also continued, and Mr.

Watson has delivered it during the past ten years (1923) in all parts of the country hundreds of times.

In the evening of October 17th, members of the Chicago Telephone Company gave a musical comedy at the Stude-baker Theatre in honor of the Pioneers. It was called "Telephonery" and in two acts presented with farce and impersonation and delightful humor the past and the two-hundred-year-distant future of the art. The past was pro-duced, or reproduced by A. P. Allen, M. D. Atwater, and E. H. Bangs. The future came full fledged from the imagi-nation of Angus S. Hibbard. Yet both acts had in them the essential of good caricature, something of truth or probability. Of this the Bell Telephone News said:

"At the risk of being called the death's head at the feast, we venture to suggest another serious thought in connection with the wholly ad-mirable and almost wholly humorous performance. The two acts introduced scenes showing the past and future of the art of communi-cation—the present being too obvious, we presume, to require treat-ment. The second act is pure imagination and right here is the sad part. The sober truth is that any attempt to tell what the future holds for the art of communication is pure imagination and the scene in A. D. 2113, so cleverly worked out, is as liable to be a true representation of the future as anything else that might be imagined.

"For we do not know what time will bring forth. As the old Gilli-land, Williams and Berliner apparatus of a generation ago is now hope-lessly obsolete—although good for its age—so the present magnificent switchboards must inevitably yield in time to come to something better. This will not be a sudden change but a gradual evolution, the good slowly giving place to the best and that best again passing downward through the graduations of good, fair, poor, and worthless. It is the ever-recurring tragedy of telephony, turned for an hour into comedy, but going on endlessly even while the actors in the little play trod the boards."

On Saturday, October 18th, the visiting Pioneers were first taken for a visit to the building of the Central Union Telephone Company, and then by automobile to the Western Electric Company's plant at Hawthorne. Here after a visit to part of the works luncheon was served. A ball game between nines of the Western Electric Company and the Chicago Telephone Company resulted in a tie of 3–3 after ten innings. In the evening the Convention closed with a memorable banquet in the Gold Room of the Congress Hotel.

Preparations for the Convention were in charge of a General Committee of Arrangements consisting of A. S. Hibbard, H. F. Hill, and F. A. Ketcham, with other committees under them.

In its three years the Telephone Pioneers of America had attained a membership of 1183. It had reached maturity and size, and its character had become well defined. It was an established institution, able and ready to exert its influence and to render service.

THE MEETING IN RICHMOND

For their Fourth Annual Convention the Telephone Pioneers of America accepted the invitation of the Chesapeake & Potomac Company to hold the meetings at Richmond, Virginia. The Convention was accordingly called together by Vice President Thomas D. Lockwood, on the morning of Wednesday, October 29, 1914, at the Hotel Jefferson in that city. Mr. J. W. Crews, Vice President of the Company presented to the audience the Mayor of Richmond, the Hon. George A. Ainslie, who cordially welcomed the Pioneers to the city in behalf of the people of Richmond.

The morning session was taken up with the usual routine reports. No special questions came up for action. Henry W. Pope, the father of the Telephone Pioneers and since the beginning the Secretary of the organization, was unable on account of serious illness to be present. His report was presented and his other duties performed by Roswell H. Starrett, as Acting Secretary. A telegram of sympathy and cheer was sent to Mr. Pope by the Convention with hope for his speedy recovery. Mr. Pope died however a little more than a year later, on February 29, 1916.

In the election of officers for the succeeding year the following Pioneers were chosen: President, Theodore N. Vail; Vice Presidents, Thomas D. Lockwood, Thomas B. Doolittle, Angus S. Hibbard, and George E. McFarland; Treasurer, George D. Milne; Executive Committee, Charles E. Scribner, Edgar F. Sherwood, and James T. Moran. The appointive members were Charles G. DuBois and James Robb. On account of continued illness, Mr. Pope resigned the office of

R. H. STARRETT, *Secretary* since
January 1, 1915

Secretary and the Executive Committee chose R. H. Starrett in his place.

The speaking of the afternoon session began with a contribution to the historical material being gathered by the Telephone Pioneers in a paper on "Pioneer Telephone Train Despatching," by J. S. McCulloh. He gave his remembrances of the first use of the telephone for this purpose in January, 1882, on the Athens Branch of the West Shore Railroad. Although very successful, this was an isolated instance, and no distinct advance was made in train handling by means of the telephone until about 20 years later.

In another brief address Angus S. Hibbard put safely on record the facts surrounding his designing of the emblem of the Telephone, the Blue Bell, and its adoption for long distance telephony by Edward J. Hall, Jr., for the American Telephone and Telegraph Company on January 5, 1889. It was also brought out that the badge of the Telephone Pioneers was designed by Henry W. Pope. To this a distinctive feature is added each year.

The outstanding address of this Convention was by Nathaniel T. Guernsey, on The Relation of the American Telephone & Telegraph Company to the Telephone Business. Mr. Guernsey laid down the proposition that the relation of the American Telephone & Telegraph Company to the Associated Companies is not an artificial one but grows out of

The Capitol
Richmond

the original need and nature of the work. The famous fifth claim of the original Bell patent, he said, announced the discovery of new territory which theretofore had not only been unexplored and undeveloped, but absolutely unknown.

"The undertaking which confronted the telephone pioneers when Mr. Vail became manager in 1878 was enormous. What they undertook to do was to transform the immense undeveloped potentialities of the telephone into a concrete, commercially practical and theretofore unknown public service. These circumstances, and not any man or collection of men, determined what must be the relations of the American Telephone & Telegraph Company and its predecessors to the telephone business, if the great discovery of Dr. Bell was to be utilized and if the public was to derive from it the potential benefits which it offered.

How the function of the American Telephone & Telegraph Company as the central, creative, fostering and balancing organization operates in the various phases of telephone work he proceeded to show in a comprehensive explanation of what the American Company did for the Associated Companies, department by department,—the General Staff, the Accounting Department, the Legal, the Patent, the Engineering Department; and also the Western Electric Company. The impression he gave of the solidarity of the Bell System as a great federated unit was incontrovertible. As an illustration of this he cited the conditions at the time of the storm in Ohio and Indiana, in 1912:

"Instantly, every resource of the Western Electric Company was expended to aid the effort to restore the service. There was no question as to whether the necessary material was available; it was available, and shipments started immediately from the nearest supply depots. There was no question as to increased prices because of the extraordinary

emergency demands; the regular prices prevailed. There were no questions as to credit or terms; the credit existed, and the terms were normal. There was prompt, efficient, smoothly working cooperation in an
emergency, done normally as a part of the day's work, because it is a
part of the service which belongs to the Associated Companies."

The special significance of Mr. Guernsey's address to
the Telephone Pioneers was that the Bell System itself, and
as a whole, today, is pioneer in essential character. Con-
vincingly and specifically he built up the picture of the
great corporate pioneer till his hearers almost saw him
standing like a man, his various members all working
together harmoniously and efficiently. Then he turned
suddenly in his last paragraph to point out the task that
great corporate pioneer has before him:

"It is natural that the first generation of telephone pioneers, looking
back upon the marvelous achievements of less than forty years, should
feel that what can be accomplished has been accomplished, should feel
that there is little to add, except in the way of refinements, to a telephone
service that is approaching in scope the limits of the imagination of its
founders, and that in efficiency and accuracy is the model of the world.
But this is a delusion to which each generation in its wisdom has been
subject. It is a mistake. There always remains more to be done than
has been done; the possibilities of the future are greater than the accomplishments of the past."

The Convention banquet was held that same evening,
Thursday, October 29th, at the Hotel Jefferson, Richmond.
The following morning the Pioneers took steamboat for the
trip down the James River to Jamestown and then on to
Old Point Comfort, where dinner was served at the Cham-
berlin Hotel. Here the Pioneers had the pleasure of being
greeted by Mr. Vail, who met them at the wharf and also
joined them at the dinner. During the night the Pioneers

went by boat to Washington. On Saturday they had an enjoyable sight-seeing trip about the Capital City.

There were two Committees of Arrangements for this Convention, the General Committee under the chairmanship of F. H. Bethell, and the Local Committee under the chairmanship of J. W. Crews.

The Meeting in San Francisco

: The Panama-Pacific Exposition brought the Telephone Pioneers to San Francisco in 1915. There they assembled at the St. Francis Hotel, on Tuesday, September 21st. Vice President Thomas D. Lockwood presided at the morning session. The Hon. James Rolph, Jr., in an eloquent and cordial speech welcomed the Pioneers to San Francisco; and Mr. H. T. Scott extended the welcome of the Pacific Telephone & Telegraph Company.

In the transaction of business the By-Laws, Section 10, were amended to the effect that any member who failed to pay the annual dues for two years shall thereby forfeit membership, but might be reinstated on payment of all arrears.

In the election of officers for the year 1916, the following Pioneers were chosen, as customary Mr. Vail being elected by a separate ballot: President, Theodore N. Vail; Vice Presidents, Thomas D. Lockwood, A. S. Hibbard, T. B.

The St. Francis Hote.

Doolittle, and L. B. McFarlane; Treasurer, George D. Milne; Executive Committee, Edgar F. Sherwood, F. A. Pickernell, Charles G. DuBois. The appointive members were Albert L. Salt and Richard T. McComas. The Executive Committee elected Roswell H. Starrett to be Secretary.

At the afternoon session, as Mr. Lockwood was one of the speakers he asked Charles G. DuBois to take the chair. The three addresses were all of them, as Mr. Lockwood called to the attention of the Pioneers at the end of the meeting, of distinctively historical or reminiscent character. All of them placed on record material which otherwise might easily have been lost to the annals of telephony.

In the first address Thomas D. Lockwood presented a valuable paper on The Forerunners and Genesis of the Telephone Exchange. Emphasizing the importance of the telephone exchange by the statement by him in the Boston Electrical Handbook, that

"While it is the telephone that has made the telephone exchange possible, it is the exchange that has made the telephone indispensable."

he reviewed the history of exchanges from the first British patent for an electric telegraph exchange granted to the Frenchman, F. M. A. Dumont, down to the telegraph exchanges of the Gold and Stock Telegraph Company, in New York, in 1869, that of Henry Bentley in Philadelphia, which grew into the Philadelphia Local Telegraph Company, and that of the Law Telegraph Company, organized by William A. Childs in New York, in 1874 or 1875. After the inception of the telephone as a means of communication, he described the experimental telephone exchanges of the

Holmes Burglar Alarm Company in Boston in 1877, the
plans which John Ponton of Titusville, Pennsylvania, prepared for exchange service in the same year, the private
telephone exchange that Isaac D. Smith of Hartford, Connecticut, arranged to connect his drug store with the offices
of the physicians who patronized him, and the Bridgeport
Social Telegraph Company exchange which was organized
by Thomas B. Doolittle, all in the same year. These led up
to the regular commercial telephone exchanges, the first of
which, he said was finished on January 28, 1878, and opened
for business on February 1, at New Haven, Connecticut,
and the second on February 14, 1878, at Meriden, Connecticut. Mr. Lockwood's paper was printed in full at the end
of the Proceedings of the 1915 Convention together with
an addendum on the general advance of the telephone
business.

The next address was by C. B. Hopkins on Early Telephone Experiences on the Pacific Coast. Mr. Hopkin's
account of his experiences in the Indian days in Washington
Territory, of the first telephones he ever saw in 1883, and the
way he acquired and built up the C. B. Hopkins Telephone
System and his troubles with "Bee Hive Joe," ending an
extra-territorial concession from the American Bell Telephone Company made a most interesting story.

The last address was a paper by Henry W. Pope, A
Retrospect of the Application of Electricity to Local Pur-
poses Prior to the Telephone. As Mr. Pope was prevented
by his illness from being present, his paper was read to the
Convention by Mr. Lockwood. Mr. Pope's and Mr.
Lockwood's addresses were complementary to each other.
Mr. Pope treated the early telegraph systems also but leading

up to the work of the American District Telegraph Company, of which he was at one time the General Superintendent in New York City. He made clear the fact that the Telephone benefited considerably by the excellent training the American District Telegraph Company gave its men and interspersed his more serious outline of development with so many delightful anecdotes and characterizations that the paper was rich in human quality as well as in historical value. The Convention sent Mr. Pope a telegram of thanks and good wishes.

The Exposition itself, the trip to San Francisco and the trip home again comprehended abundant entertainment in connection with the Convention, so much in fact that it is impossible to enumerate all of even the special features. The Convention banquet was held the evening of Tuesday, September 21st, at the St. Francis. On Wednesday the Pioneers spent the day on a trip to Mt. Tamalpais and the Muir Woods. Thursday was spent at the Exposition Grounds. Friday and Saturday every one did as he chose. On Sunday, September 26th, the Pioneers resumed their journey home, going by way of Southern California. Among the special attractions must be mentioned the personal demonstration of the new Transcontinental Telephone Line. Every Pioneer was offered an opportunity to talk with his own home. A commemorative bronze medal was presented by the Directors of the Exposition to the Association, and the Pacific Telephone & Telegraph Company presented every Pioneer with a souvenir paper weight of California redwood and bronze.

There were two Committees in charge of the Arrangements for the San Francisco Convention, the General Committee under the chairmanship of George E. McFarland, and the Local Committee under that of D. P. Fullerton.

THE MEETING IN ATLANTA

For the Sixth Annual Convention of the Telephone Pioneers, the last meeting before the United States went into the war, the hospitality of Atlanta, Georgia, and of the Southern Bell Telephone Company was accepted. In the Piedmont Hotel, Atlanta, on the morning of Friday, October 27, 1916, the Convention was called to order by Vice President Thomas D. Lockwood. The Hon. James G. Woodward, Mayor of Atlanta, graciously welcomed the Pioneers to the city, and J. Epps Brown extended to them the welcome of the Southern Bell Telephone Company.

The only special question arising in the transaction of business was the suggestion that a life membership be es-tablished in the organization. This was presented to the meeting in proper form and referred to the Executive Com-mittee for consideration and for report to the next meeting.

When the election of officers for the en-suing year was taken up, Charles G. Du-Bois, as Chairman of the Nominating Com-mittee prefaced the report of the Commit-tee with some clarify-ing remarks which were well received:

"Since the appointment of the Nominating Committee some ten minutes ago, we have carefully canvassed the entire membership of the Association, consisting of some fourteen hundred members, I believe, and have given careful consideration to those who are best entitled to serve the Association as its officers for the coming year. We had a number of disputes on the subject, as you may have noticed in our meeting, but finally with a get-together spirit we came to an agreement on the following nominations, which I now present:

"For President (and I desire to say that we had no controversy as to this): Mr. Theo. N. Vail." (Applause.)

As usual the Secretary was unanimously instructed to cast a separate ballot for Mr. Vail. The result of the election showed the following list of officers for the next year, 1917: President, Theodore N. Vail; Vice Presidents, Thomas D. Lockwood, Edgar F. Sherwood, James T. Moran, Ben S. Read; Treasurer, George D. Milne; Executive Committee, Frank A. Pickernell, Richard T. McComas, Albert L. Salt. The members appointed by the Chair were James Robb and Charles H. Wilson. The Executive Committee reelected R. H. Starrett to be Secretary.

The afternoon session brought a number of speakers to the interested attention of the Pioneers. In the first address L. B. McFarlane gave reminiscences of the early days of the telephone in Canada. Canadians have always felt a special pride in the telephone because, as Dr. Bell said, Brantford was his thinking place. Mr. McFarlane touched on many of the beginnings of telephone work in different parts of Canada, from Mr. Bell's assignment of a large interest in the Canadian patents to his father, the signing of the first anticipative telephone contract at Hamilton, Ontario, the rather sporadic beginnings at St. John, New Brunswick, Ottawa, and Montreal, to the appearance of the

Bell Telephone of Canada in 1880, and the extension of the system to Newfoundland in 1883. The true conditions of the early work were summarized by Mr. McFarlane with delightful brevity.

"The writer was appointed Superintendent of the Telephone Department of the Dominion Telegraph Company when the patents were acquired. Upon asking for instructions and information as to his duties he was told to go and find out, that being all the lead they could give him."

The effect of affiliation with the American telephone system on the isolated exchanges and precarious conditions of the telephone in Canada was also vividly suggested.

"Our honored President, Mr. T. N. Vail, had been a director of the Bell Company of Canada from its inception and his advice was sought. After studying the situation for a few minutes, he called for a map of the Provinces of Quebec and Ontario and with a blue pencil drew lines from Montreal to various Canadian cities and towns within a radius of 300 miles. The Manager, whose longest toll line barely exceeded 20 miles, gasped when Mr. Vail remarked, 'Build Long Distance lines at once to connect all the exchanges within this territory.' 'But,' objected the Manager, 'they will not pay.' To this Mr. Vail responded 'I did not say they would, but they will unify and save your business.' "

The address of F. H. Bethell gathered together and presented much valuable material of the history of the Chesapeake & Potomac Telephone Company.

Mr. Bethell began by expressing appreciative acknowledgment of the historical research done by P. G. Burton in the preparation of the paper. His story began with the time when George C. Maynard, "the builder," became the agent of the Bell interests in Washington, D. C., and went on through the formation of the National Telephone Exchange in 1879, and of the National Capital Telephone

Company in 1881, to the organization of the Chesapeake & Potomac Telephone Company in 1883. Similarly he told of the beginnings in Baltimore from the time of A. G. Davis and J. H. C. Watts. His account of struggles and progress was sometimes amusing, as in the obliteration of telephone service in Washington, in 1880, and sometimes most instructive, as in his account of the celebrated Manning Case which was decided in the U. S. Supreme Court and the consequent legislation by Congress in 1902 and 1904, always interesting, and even thrilling in his tribute to the heroism of the telephone girls in the Baltimore fire of February 7, 1904.

Another valuable paper was that contributed by F. A. Pickernell, read in his absence by Mr. Lockwood, about the testing of the Van Rysselberghe system in the spring of 1890 and its emergency success at the time of the sleet storm of April 2–3, 1891, between Boston and New York, in consequence of which it was introduced into the telephone system under the name of the Composite system. Incidents were also submitted, and printed in the Proceedings,—about the first installation of a telephone exchange in San Diego, California, in 1882, by J. W. Thompson; and about a telephone demonstration in New Bedford, Massachusetts, in 1878, by B. Franklin Wordell.

It is no depreciation of other papers to say that the address of Charles E. Scribner on The Genesis of the Telephone Multiple Switchboard was one of the most important of the papers presented at these Conventions. Authoritative in substance and historical in method of presentation, it is a concise primer of his work and that of his associates in the development of the switchboard. Mr. Scribner ex-

pressed appreciation of assistance rendered in the preparation of the paper by F. J. Holmes.   In Mr. Scribner's
absence, the paper was read by Kendall Weisiger.

With three steps Mr. Scribner led into his subject.

"The telephone was placed on the market in 1877, commercial telephone exchange service established January 28, 1878, and the first multiple switchboard installed in January, 1879, in the 'Edison' telephone
exchange of the American District Telegraph Company, at 118 La Salle
Street, Chicago."

As an introduction, Mr. Scribner then gave a résumé of
pre-telephone switchboards touching ground which had
already been dealt with in addresses by Mr. Lockwood and
Mr. Pope at other Pioneer meetings, but summed up the
situation at the time the telephone came into the field, by
saying that

"In none of the telegraph undertakings had there appeared a suffi-
cient demand for instant and constantly changing interconnections
between lines on a large scale to be taken seriously."

The Western Electric Company began the manufacture
of telephone apparatus in 1877.   Mr. Scribner went into
the Company in January of that year and when the Company went into telephone manufacture he was assigned to
that work.

Characterizing the rapid development of telephone exchanges in response to the rapid increase in demand of the
public for telephone service, he said:

"Things moved swiftly in those days, for the telephone industry
had not more than fairly launched than subscribers increased so rapidly
and calls for connections came into the exchanges so fast that all telegraph switching facilities, which were naturally first used, proved inade-

quate, improvised modifications were almost useless and new contri-
vances of only temporary benefit. The value of the telephone exchange came to be appreciated by the public very soon and the growth
of the telephone exchange gave to its promoters surprise following surprise. A switchboard designed and well calculated to provide for the
estimated growth of years would be found of too small capacity for the
needs of the time when completed, the growth of the business between
the date of the order and that of completion being sufficiently great for
this result."

With this picture of the background conditions in
which the work went on, Mr. Scribner outlined the development of the switchboard from the initial and basic idea
of Leroy B. Firman, first constructed in 1879 and patented
in 1882, to the No. 1 Relay Board, Mr. Scribner followed
step by step the development in his masterly exposition,
according credit to his associate inventors and describing
the outstanding devices in considerable detail. It is im-
practicable to condense for this statement Mr. Scribner's
already concentrated outline, but it gives an impression of
the team-work and active cooperation which has built up
the multiple telephone switchboard to mention the names
of those beside himself who contributed to this work.
They include: L. B. Firman, Charles H. Wilson, Clark C.
Haskins, Milo G. Kellogg, J. C. Warner, E. P. Warner, F.
Shaw, J. J. Carty, J. A. Seely, E. M. Barton, R. V. Free-
man, H. B. Thayer, F. B. Cook, J. A. Cook, J. Steiner, O.
A. Bell, J. J. O'Connell, James L. McQuarrie, F. R. Mc-
Berty. And there were besides, of course, many others.
Yet in spite of the extraordinary achievement already at-
tained in the development of the switchboard Mr. Scribner
intimated in closing that this department of telephone
invention at least was still in the pioneer stage.

"We are now entering a period of important developments and pos-
sibly of radical changes in telephone switchboard practice as the result
of which there is some probability of real innovations."

And the seven years since this paper was read have
amply proven this anticipation to have been true.

The entertainment offered the Telephone Pioneers by
the people of Atlanta was typical of Southern hospitality.
Friday evening, October 27th, the banquet was held at the
Piedmont Hotel, Atlanta. The next day was devoted to
visiting telephone offices and exchanges, a barbecue at the
Druid Hills Club, and automobile drives in the vicinity.
Sunday morning the Pioneer's Special left Atlanta for
Chattanooga and a visit to the adjacent battlefields of
Chickamauga, Missionary Ridge, and Lookout Mountain,
and then proceeded to Asheville, North Carolina, where a
delightful day was spent.

An interesting souvenir was given to all the Telephone
Pioneers attending the Convention in the form of a medal
made of the first copper wire strung for long distance telephone service, between Boston and New York in the spring
of 1884.

The Committee of Arrangements consisted of J. Epps
Brown, Chairman, Barney A. Kaiser, and Albert L. Salt.
Working under them were six Local Committees.

THE MEETING IN MONTREAL

After the Atlanta Convention of 1916 there was no
meeting of the Telephone Pioneers for three years on
account of the war. When the Pioneers gathered together
again, at Montreal, in 1920, the outlook of the world was
changed. And not less in the Telephone industry than in

other walks of life. Seventy-two Pioneers had died since the roll had last been called.* Among these were promi-nent the names of John A. Barrett, Eugene M. Wilson, George Y. Wallace, George V. Leverett, Rowland G. Hazard, James C. Vail, Charles F. Sise, George C. Maynard, Edward B. Field, Sr., and Edward B. Field, Jr., Charles B. Hopkins, Edwin T. Holmes, William R. Driver, Nathan C. Kingsbury, and Theodore N. Vail. Many of these were of the first generation of Telephone Pioneers.

A most difficult situation still confronted the Telephone in America resulting from war-time conditions, in the de-pleted personnel, high cost of living and the high level of all prices, and the lack of supplies and material at any price.

Telephone men and women under Col. John J. Carty had done an extraordinary piece of pioneer work with the American Expeditionary Forces in France, and the work that needed to be done now at home to restore normal con-ditions in the telephone industry and telephone service was no less of pioneer character. It was therefore to enter into a new period of their history that the Telephone Pioneers of America met at Montreal in 1920. It was necessary for them to adjust themselves to the new demands and new conditions of a new life.

The officers elected in 1916 for the year 1917 held over until their successors should be elected. Accordingly, as Senior Vice President, Thomas D. Lockwood called the Seventh General Meeting and Annual Convention of the Telephone Pioneers of America to order at the Windsor

---

* One in 1914 and 4 in 1916 were not reported until after the proceedings for the Atlanta Convention were issued. The others were 13 in 1917; 29 in 1918; 11 in 1919; and 14 in 1920.

Hotel, Montreal, P. Q., Canada, on the morning of Friday, September 10, 1920.

His Worship, the Hon. Mederic Martin, Mayor of Montreal, was then presented to the Pioneers and he made a very cordial address of welcome to the city, which was sincerely appreciated by all present.

During the three years interim the affairs of the Association had been conducted by the Executive Committee. It had issued a report to the members in the form of a letter on November 29, 1919. There was little to add to this except that it had not seemed advisable to the Committee to institute a Life Membership in the Telephone Pioneers at the present time.

A Committee was appointed to draw up resolutions on the death of the President of the Telephone Pioneers of America, Theodore N. Vail. This Committee consisted of James Robb, A. L. Salt, and E. K. Hall. It submitted the following resolutions which were unanimously adopted by a rising vote, spread upon the minutes and sent to the family:

THEODORE N. VAIL MEMORIAL

The Telephone Pioneers of America by the death of Theodore N. Vail have lost their first President, a most distinguished member and a most beloved and devoted friend.

Born in Carroll County, Ohio, July 16th, 1854, Theodore Newton Vail had achieved national prominence when, in 1878,

*Windsor Hotel
and Mount Royal,
Montreal, Canada*

he resigned as General Superintendent of the United States Railway Mail Service, to become a pioneer in the great task of making the newly invented telephone the instrument of a nation, and a blessing to the civilized world.

As the first Executive of the Bell System he blazed the trail for us all to follow through the forest of difficulties which had to be overcome in the early years of telephone development.

He was the typical pioneer, leading the way over unknown paths, clearing up the underbrush of doubt and swamps of discouragement, until, at the end of the trail, he witnessed the realization of his early vision of a great nation-wide telephone system, serving all the people all the time, the continent spanned by the talking wire and the oceans traversed by the wireless speech.

It has been well said that
"We live in deeds, not years;
In thoughts, not breaths;
In feelings, not in figures on a dial."

And in that sense, the life of Theodore N. Vail exceeded that of the patriarchs.

A human and kindly man, he bound into one loyal family a quarter of a million of telephone men and women, and made neighbors of a hun dred million people.

The Telephone Pioneers will ever hold his memory dear, and in the years to come his life will prove an inspiration to nobler thought and higher effort on the part of every member of the great telephone family.

In the election of officers H. B. Thayer was chosen by a unanimous rising vote for the office of President, and the Secretary cast a separate ballot for him. The officers for the year 1921 were: President, H. B. Thayer; Vice Presidents, H. J. Pettengill, F. A. Stevenson, A. L. Salt, B. L. Kilgour; Treasurer, G. D. Milne; Executive Committee, James Robb, E. K. Hall, J. S. McCulloh. The appointive members of the Executive Committee were J. J. Carty and J. T. Moran. The Executive Committee reelected R. H. Starrett to the office of Secretary.

As soon as Mr. Thayer had been elected President, Vice President Thomas D. Lockwood, who was presiding, called upon L. B. McFarlane, President of the Bell Tele-phone Company of Canada, whose guests the Pioneers were, to escort the new President to the Chair.

On taking the Chair Mr. Thayer prefaced a short speech by expressing appreciation of the honor that had been conferred upon him. He then sounded the keynote of the new period in the history of the Telephone Pioneers, first with respect to his own term of office, and then with respect to the purpose of the organization as a whole.

"Talking from the experience of the country south of us, I think it is much better to announce a platform after election than before. It avoids disagreeable discussion. I have two planks of a platform: one of them is the usual plank on the other side; that is, one term for the President. I believe in rotation of officers, but will go a little farther than does this country south of us. After election I propose that there should be some legislation confining the Presidency of the Association to one term.

"My other plank is a broader and fuller career for the Pioneers. It has seemed to me that the four years in which we have not had meetings has been a twilight zone between an era that is closing and an era that is opening for the Pioneers. Reference has been made to the death of Mr. Vail and Mr. Sise. They were the two great leaders of the pioneer movement, one in the United States and one in Canada. They have passed away. We, who are also pioneers, have fallen in behind them from time to time. Pioneer expeditions moved into unknown territory. That movement into unknown territory is continuing today just as it did forty years ago. Mr. McFarlane said to me yesterday that there were as many problems today as there were forty years ago. Now between two and three hundred thousand have joined this pioneer movement, but the rules of this Association have wisely been made, that among those pioneers,—those who have been admitted to this Association were only those who have passed a substantial part of their lives in telephone work. So that being a Pioneer now means years of service in telephone work."

He closed by saying that for the year of his administration as President of the Telephone Pioneers he appointed Mr. Lockwood Perpetual Chairman.

At the opening of the afternoon session R. H. Starrett called the meeting to order. John J. Carty secured the recognition of the Chair and addressed the Pioneers.

"All the members of this Society realize what a great honor it is to be a Pioneer, and the younger men of the telephone business in the United States and Canada are looking forward to the time when they too will be eligible for admission into this Society as Telephone Pioneers. It is a great honor to be an officer of this Society, but there are also other honors connected with the Society, one of which is that any person worthy of the dignity may be created an Honorary Member. I have been asked and I am very proud to be selected as the one to perform the duty of asking your unanimous consent for the election at this meeting to Honorary Membership of four names that have always been distinguished in the history of our Society. Two of them are here in the Dominion of Canada, which has played such an important part in the development of the telephone, and two are in the United States. I, therefore, propose and ask unanimous consent for the election at this meeting to Honorary Membership of the following young gentlemen: T. D. Lockwood, L. B. McFarlane, T. B. Doolittle, K. J. Dunstan."

The four Pioneers were unanimously elected by a rising vote to Honorary Membership; Mr. Starrett formally announced their election to them; and each of them expressed his appreciation of the honor conferred upon him. Mr. Starrett then yielded the Chair to Mr. Lockwood as Perpetual Chairman.

The first speaker of the afternoon was W. H. Black. In an address of quiet eloquence he urged the importance of maintaining personal contact between officers and employes as the telephone work increased, that friendly relationship which the organization of the Telephone Pioneers fostered among telephone men and women and for which it is notable —the spirit of comradeship itself.

"We describe the group of Companies to which ours belong as Public Service Corporations. We all on occasion describe ourselves as public servants, claiming a place on a par with the employes of the State. We have exalted service until we are ready to call ourselves servants. But the real change, the real advance is that we are no longer officers and servants, but all alike serve. Serve our Company, serve our shareholders, serve our subscribers and serve the whole miscellaneous public which may demand or require service at our hands. It is very important that this idea of service as the common lot, the universal privilege, should permeate all ranks. The executive officers should realize the problems of the gang and the force should dismiss the idea, if they have it, that a position which carries with it a private office and a swivel chair is one entirely free from carking care. And yet, while there is greater need than ever for cooperation and concert all along the line, the fact is that the separation of the executive and the gang as far as actual business contact is concerned, is increasing all the time. Today with functional organization and the subdivision of authority and action and responsibility into Departments, Divisions and Districts, the personal touch between the executive and the man in the front line trench is difficult to maintain. But if the direct personal touch is absent, it is vitally necessary that there should be evidence of personal interest. Let us not lose the human touch amid the routines, but realize that there is a man on the job at all points."

The second address, by James H. Winfield, was historical in character although the events narrated occurred not long ago. He gave some interesting and unusual information about the Province of Nova Scotia, the Long Wharf of America, as he called it, and about the City of Halifax and its telephone equipment. He then told of the tremendous explosion in the harbor of Halifax on the morning of December 6, 1917, of the storms that followed, rendering relief work almost impossible, of the destruction in the city, the damage to the telephone plant and the quick recovery they made by dint of heroic work and cooperation with each other as well as with the assistance of outside communities. The Telephone Company was just ready to open its new exchange "Sackville" two days later, when the explosion wrecked much of the building and made difficult repairs necessary. Nonetheless the cut-over was made and the new exchange was ready to help in the emergency need for service only two weeks later, on December 21st. He closed with grateful reference to the assistance sent to Halifax by the sister Telephone Companies of New Brunswick and New England and the Bell Telephone Company of Canada.

The last speaker of the day was E. K. Hall. At the time it was impossible for Mr. Hall to take the platform as he was engaged in other duties. Mr. Lockwood therefore entertained the Pioneers with a whimsical allegory of his own invention about The Four Benevolent Giants of mythical or modern times, Aquadynamicus, Boreolzephyrus, Calhydrogenius and Elektron, until Mr. Hall came.

Mr. Lockwood's allegory proved to be a peculiarly fitting introduction to Mr. Hall's speech, which may be described as a ringing call upon the benevolent giant Elektron in the person of the Telephone Pioneers to bring into play his greatest gift to mankind, the nation-wide spirit of neighborliness and comradeship.

Taking as his text Mr. Thayer's second plank for a broader and fuller career for the Telephone Pioneers, Mr. Hall stressed the same need that Mr. Black had emphasized in urging personal contact between individual officers and employes in the Telephone Companies. But Mr. Hall took an even broader, deeper view of the matter. He declared that such personal contact, friendship and confidence must be the fundamental principle and policy of all telephone work throughout the Bell System and acclaimed such a spirit of team-work as the only thing that could solve the problems that lie before the Telephone industry, and every other industry, in the necessary adjustment to after-war conditions.

To give really good first class service, always the great problem of the telephone industry, depends absolutely on close personal relationship between the workers, on team-work—which the first pioneers had. This Mr. Hall brought home with great effect.

"This question is under discussion from one end of the world to the other, and yet the answer ought not to be difficult. It is simply a question of bringing back into industry the human contacts, the human sympathies, the closer human relations and mutual confidence which naturally existed in industry before it became necessary to conduct industries in such large units in order to lower the cost of production and render to society a larger and more extended service. To the extent that this human element has been crowded out by the rapid growth of the Bell System we are going to put it back. You Pioneers found it here when you came into the Company. You have helped to preserve it to a wonderful degree. Through your efforts and those of thousands of your associates it has been preserved to a far greater degree than in most other industries. The great growth of the business, however, the necessity of departmentalizing so much of the work and the fact that we must spread ourselves over an entire continent, all tend to make it difficult to preserve the contacts and acquaintances upon which mutual confidence and understanding so largely depend."

In closing Mr. Hall focused upon the Telephone Pioneers as a body the responsibility of bringing to present day problems the same pioneer spirit of comradeship that solved the problems of the early days.

"You Pioneers are the very people to see to it that in this great family of ours—a quarter of a million of us—there is acquaintance, friendship and confidence all the way up and down the line. We are banking on you Pioneers, and with your help we are going to show the industrial world that there is at least one inseparable industrial family."

The banquet, in the Rose Room of the Windsor Hotel, the same evening, Friday, September 10th, was a most enjoyable occasion, with special Canadian features. It was opened by the entrance of the President of the Telephone Pioneers, H. B. Thayer, with the President of the Bell Telephone Company of Canada, L. B. McFarlane, preceded by a bag-piper. On reaching their seats, Mr. Thayer proposed the toast, "To the King," which was drunk by all standing, followed by all singing, "God Save the King!" Mr. McFarlane then responded with the toast, "To the President of the United States," after which a stanza of "America" was sung. The relations of exceptional friendliness between the two nations, thus evidenced, was strikingly expressed also by J. J. Carty in one of the after-dinner speeches.

"Every telephone that has been installed in Canada and every telephone that has been installed in the United States has been an agency of good understanding and feeling between these two separate governments. This border line is unique among all nations. Instead of having a line throughout of forts, we have only a few Customs Houses. And the rest of the border we are bending back and forth with telephone and telegraph wires. I think that the cooperation between the telephone men of Canada and those of the United States is a perfect example of how these two great countries can always live side by side, connected by that link working for the common cause of civilization. So long as the Pioneers and so long as our telephone system, so long as our ideal in the work that we are engaged in goes on, so long are we assured of ever-lasting friendship and peace between Canada and the United States."

The visit of the Telephone Pioneers to Montreal was made most delightful to every one of them. Every facility that hospitality could suggest was put at their disposal for enjoying the city with its interesting historic sites and the beautiful scenery of the mountain and the environs.

In memory of Mr. Vail a bronze medal was presented by the American Telephone & Telegraph Company to every Pioneer attending the Montreal Convention. On the obverse was a portrait of Mr. Vail surrounded by the words, "Theodore Newton Vail: He made neighbors of a hundred million people;" on the reverse was a suitable inscription of presentation surrounded with a ring of tele-phone receivers.

The Committee of Arrangements in charge of the Mon-treal Convention consisted of L. B. McFarlane, Chairman, A. D. Salt, and B. A. Kaiser, with a General Committee and ten other committees working under them.

THE MEETING IN ST. LOUIS

The Eighth General Meeting of the Telephone Pioneers of America met at the Hotel Statler, St. Louis, Missouri, on the morning of Monday, October 25, 1921. The President, H. B. Thayer, called the meeting to order, and then delivered his Presidential Address on the subject of Human Progress and the Telephone. In this address Mr. Thayer discussed the place of the telephone in the history of transportation and communication and the relation of telephone work to the general scheme of world progress. The result of the introduction of the telephone into American life, he said, was that

"There is more consultation with one another; more desire for fuller information, whether of private business or state policy; more regard for the opinions of others; more unity of spirit in the United States."

The picture Mr. Thayer drew for the Pioneers was consequently one of great responsibility.

"For the present efficiency and the future development of the telephone, we are responsible to the nation. There is no other system than the Bell Telephone System that at all compares with it in the extent of its service and of its responsibility. Indeed there is no other system of any kind in the field of public utilities that carries the entire responsibility for a national service. American commerce depends upon the perfection of that service, and in a considerable measure world commerce does too. In addition to this extensive and powerful range of responsibility of the telephone and of its servants, there is no public service

Eads Bridge
St. Louis

that enters so thoroughly and so intimately into the daily life of the people. It is ours, as opportunity and as responsibility. To carry on the work to a still more perfect service is your privilege, and the privilege of your associates and successors. And, furthermore, it is your great responsibility."

The most important matter in the business session was the Report of the Executive Committee. This was presented by E. K. Hall. Taking the cue from Mr. Thayer's suggestions at Montreal that the days of pioneering never stop, the purpose of the Report was to make suggestions for such additions to the scope and plan of the Telephone Pioneers organization as to make it possible to recognize the pioneering that is going on today and that was going on ten years ago as well as the pioneering of the men who started the industry; to gather into the membership all those who are eligible; and to organize the entire 21 year personnel of the Bell System into an active and working body for leadership in the industry.

To this end a number of amendments to the Constitution and ByLaws were proposed. The more important are here noted. Article I of the Constitution was revised so as to include pioneer service during the development as well as during the inception of the telephone industry; reading

"This Association is formed for the purpose of the promotion, renewal and continuance of the friendships and fellowships made during the progress of the telephone industry between those interested therein, recalling and perpetuating the facts, traditions and memories attaching to the development of the telephone industry and the telephone system; preserving the names and records of the participants in the establishment and extension of this great system of electrical intercommunication;

and the encouragement of such other meritorious objects consistent with the foregoing as may be desirable.".

To Article II, Membership, was added a Section 2, providing that any person, regardless of the time of service or length of service, regardless also of whether now in the telephone service or not may be elected to membership by the unanimous vote of the Executive Committee, thus leaving the door open for any who have rendered special service beneficial to the telephone industry. A new Article provided for the organization of a General Assembly, to be formed of delegates from the local chapters elsewhere provided for. This was done by authorizing the establishment of a Chapter of the Telephone Pioneers in any State, Territory, Province, City or locality on application to and approval by the Executive Committee. The election of officers was delegated to the General Assembly, which would equally represent all the members, not only those who were in attendance at the Convention. The suggestion of Mr. Thayer that "no person should be elected to or occupy the office of President for more than one year," was also included in the same Article. The By-Laws, Section 10, were amended so as to make the dues $3.00 the first year and $2.00 thereafter, instead of $5.00 the first year and $2.00 thereafter.

On motion duly seconded the Convention voted to accept the Report of the Executive Committee and to adopt the amendments to the Constitution and By-Laws with but one dissenting vote. As soon as a point which had been misunderstood was explained the dissenting vote was withdrawn, making the adoption unanimous. Active discussion followed, manifesting the interest in the new

Constitution. This clarified many points and revealed the great improvements in the working of Telephone Pioneer affairs that would result from the changes.

In the election of officers the following Pioneers were chosen: President, John J. Carty; Senior Vice President, F. A. Stevenson; Vice Presidents, B. L. Kilgour, C. H. Rottger, J. J. Robinson; Executive Committee, T. P. Sylvan, John H. Passman, Miss Mary T. Reuse, B. A. Kaiser, J. E. Warren. Under the new Constitution and By-Laws there were no appointive members of the Executive Committee. R. H. Starrett was elected Secretary by the Executive Committee and F. A. Buttrick, Treasurer. The newly elected President, J. J. Carty, was escorted to the Chair and expressed appreciation of the honor conferred upon him in a brief address.

For the Monday afternoon session the Convention adjourned to the out-door Municipal Theatre of St. Louis in Forest Park. There a demonstration of the Bell Loud Speaker was prepared for the Pioneers by a staff in charge of W. D. Pomeroy of the American Telephone & Telegraph Company. H. J. Pettengill presided.

The speakers were Lieut. Governor Hiram Lloyd of Missouri, Hon. Henry W. Kiel, Mayor of St. Louis, E. D. Nims, B. S. Read, H. B. Thayer, and J. J. Carty. Col. Carty contrasted the beginnings of telephone research with the large staff and remarkable equipment which had produced the Loud Speaker.

"In the beginning our laboratories consisted of a small room with only two workers; one of those workers was Alexander Graham Bell, the inventor of the telephone itself. He was the first pioneer. The other

JOHN J. CARTY

worker was Thomas A. Watson, who, acting under the instructions of
Bell, made the first instrument and heard the first words. The one-
room laboratory, with its two workers has increased until today it
occupies the entire building which was until recently pointed out with
pride as the great factory of the Western Electric Company; and today
that is scarcely large enough to contain the laboratory alone; and the
workers now number more than 2800. So we may pay a tribute here
today to these younger men who are actually doing pioneer work now.
These young men, hundreds—I might say, thousands of them, are
present with us in spirit, and it is on their behalf that I can offer as a
tribute at this meeting this apparatus."

Col. Carty had also brought with him an exact reproduction of Dr. Bell's first telephone. This was connected
in on the circuit and Col. Carty spoke through it and the
Loud Speaker to the assembled audience, as he said, "to
show the wonderful work that was done by those old
Pioneers and the achievements of these young Pioneers
who are today qualifying themselves by their efforts and
accomplishments to be real Pioneers in this Society."

On Tuesday automobile drives about St. Louis and
through its beautiful park system brought the Pioneers to
the Riverview Club for luncheon as the guests of the Western Electric Company. In the evening the Pioneers were
the guests as usual of the American Telephone & Telegraph
Company at the banquet at the Statler. A programme of
entertainment took the place of the customary after-dinner
speeches, including an allegorical dramatic performance of
which the cast represented Capital, Plant, Public Relations,
and a little tot representing Net Earnings. Each Pioneer
received as a souvenir a copy of Albert Bigelow Paine's
biography of Theodore N. Vail, entitled In One Man's
Life, specially bound for the occasion.

The Committee of Arrangements for the St. Louis Convention consisted of H. J. Pettengill, Chairman, F. A.
Stevenson, B. A. Kaiser, and J. S. McCulloh, with a General
Committee and eleven special committees working under
them.

THE MEETING IN CLEVELAND

The Telephone Pioneers met for the first time under
their new Constitution at Cleveland, Ohio, on Friday,
September 29, 1922. The President, J. J. Carty, called the
first meeting of the General Assembly to order in the
Hotel Cleveland and the Secretary called the roll by chapters and delegates. There were 19 chapters represented,
and an attendance of 65.

Before taking up the business to be transacted, General
Carty called the attention
of the delegates to the importance of this repre-
sentative and legislative
body of the Telephone
Pioneers.

"Here we have to pre-
pare for the great work of
this Society, and its greatest work is to build up,
sustain, carry on, transmit
the ideals of our service.

"We delegates are
here now for very serious
purposes. We have a very
great responsibility. The
great body of Pioneers has
turned over to you, ladies

The Monument.

and gentlemen, all of its powers.   You have power to amend the
Constitution; you elect the officers; you direct our activities.   They
have such confidence in you that to you they have entrusted all of
these great responsibilities.   So that today marks a new departure in
the history of our Society."

The Senior Vice President, F. A. Stevenson, presented
the recommendations of the Executive Committee for certain amendments to the Constitution and By-Laws in order
to carry out better the intent of the recent revision.   These
covered such matters as a specific definition of the membership of the General Assembly; the fixing of the fiscal year
to coincide with the calendar year; that the term of officers
shall begin on the January 1st next after their election;
overlapping terms for members of the Executive Committee; and that a retiring President shall be a member
ex-officio of the Executive Committee for one year following his term of office.   All these amendments were after
interesting discussion unanimously passed.

Free general discussion after these amendments were
passed brought out suggestions for other amendments.
After the ideas of the delegates present had been expressed
on them they were referred to the Executive Committee
for consideration and report at the next meeting of the
General Assembly.   Among these suggested amendments
were: the reelection of a President for a second term;
and provision ensuring the attendance of the presidents
of chapters at the annual meetings.

In the election the following Pioneers were chosen as
officers for the year 1923: President, Leonard H. Kinnard;
Senior Vice President, F. A. Stevenson; Vice Presidents,
James T. Moran, J. A. Stewart, E. A. Reed; Executive

LEONARD H. KINNARD

Committee, (one year) B. A. Kaiser, J. E. Warren; (two years) Verne Ray, Miss Mary Miller, E. K. Hall. In accordance with the new Constitution, both the Treasurer and the Secretary were chosen by the Executive Committee. F. A. Buttrick and R. H. Starrett being continued in office.

At the meeting of the Telephone Pioneer Association in the afternoon the Secretary read the report of the General Assembly on the transactions of their meeting. The Secretary also reported that at the time of the meeting the membership of the Association had increased by 1,913 during the year to 4,276.

The Mayor of Cleveland, the Hon. Fred Kohler, came to greet the Pioneers and bid them welcome to the city in the name of the people of Cleveland. The President-elect, L. H. Kinnard, at this time arrived at the Convention and briefly expressed his appreciation of the honor conferred upon him.

The President of the Telephone Pioneers, John J. Carty, then delivered his Presidential Address, Ideals of the Telephone Service, a Tribute to the Memory of Alexander Graham Bell. General Carty recalled to the Pioneers the first meeting of the Telephone Pioneers eleven years before, in Boston, the birthplace of the telephone. He reminded them that Alexander Graham Bell was present on that occasion, and how with cordial modesty he had said to them:

"I feel it a little presumptuous on my part to try to speak of the telephone to telephone men. You have all gone so far beyond me. It is to you that this great telephone development is due. I belong to the past; you belong to the present."

General Carty then briefly reviewed Dr. Bell's life and the rapid development of the telephone which he lived to see, to the dramatic moment of the Burial of the Unknown American Soldïer.

"On that day the achievements of science imparted a mystical power to the most solemn national ceremony in the history of America. This ceremony, its deep significance so enriched by the art of Bell, we can now believe contained an exalted sanction of the greatest of all the achievements of his life. These are but some of the advances which have been made in the first half century of the telephone art, which is now drawing to a close. They belong to the golden age of communica-tions, which has achieved the extension of the spoken word throughout both space and time. But this golden age has not yet ended, and when we contemplate the possibilities of the future we discover that it has only just begun. It is to the future that we must now turn our minds and direct our endeavors. It is true that we belong to the past, but it is equally true that we belong to the present. The greatest work which our Society can do is to exemplify the ideals of our service, and to trans-mit to its future members the splendid traditions of our art. They rest upon a solid basis of achievement and represent the practical purpose of that great telephone system of intercommunication which bears the name of our First Pioneer."

The peculiar importance of electrical communications in the social organism was first appreciated by biologists. Herbert Spencer spoke of the telegraph as the nervous sys-tem of society. The development of this idea General Carty traced in terms of the present day, when the tele-phone has supplied a much more apt element as the ner-vous system of human society than the telegraph ever could have. Confirmed by the writings of the latest authoritative biologists, General Carty made a comparison between the building up of the human body from cell units and the building up of the social whole of mankind from the units of individual men and women. In that ideal future society what will be the place of the communications system? To

be the nervous system of Mankind, the center and means of
intelligence and of human progress, was General Carty's
reply. In the illumination of such thought, the destiny of
the telephone is indeed high and its career only just begun.

"Here we have portrayed the forward march of humanity toiling
ever onward to attain its goal. The realization that their wonderful art
is destined to play such an important part in this final attainment opens
up a never-ending source of power and inspiration for telephone men
and women everywhere. It adds new dignity to their calling. Already,
as we have seen, the human voice has been carried with the speed of
light across the Atlantic Ocean, and across our continent, and far out
into the Pacific; but still greater things are to come. It is the mission of
the Pioneers and their successors, and their associates among all the
nations, to build up a telephone system extending to every part of the
world, connecting together all the people of the earth. I believe that
the art which was founded by Alexander Graham Bell, our First Pioneer,
will provide the means for transmitting throughout the earth a great
voice proclaiming the dawn of a new era in which will be realized that
grandest of all our earthly aspirations—the brotherhood of man."

Asked by Mrs. Bell to express to the Telephone Pioneers and to all the men and women of the Telephone her
deep appreciation of their sympathy in her loss by the
death of Dr. Bell, and to tell them how highly Dr. Bell
valued the telephone and how proud he was of the achievements of his successors, General Carty did so by reading to
the Pioneers some letters and telegrams which he had received from Mrs. Bell. Beautiful and simple in themselves
these were listened to with impressive silence.* It was
unanimously voted that the President send a telegram to
Mrs. Bell from the Convention, and the following resolu-

*It may here be added that not long after this, on December 27, 1922, the Executive
Committee, acting in behalf of the Telephone Pioneers, elected Mrs. Bell to Honorary
Membership in their Society.

tions were also adopted unanimously by a rising vote and spread upon the minutes.

WHEREAS, The Pioneer of Telephone Pioneers, Alexander Graham Bell, after a long and noble life, has departed, leaving us, as our heritage, an example of service to mankind which all should emulate,

THEREFORE, We, Telephone Pioneers of America, in Convention assembled, realizing that time will not dim the memory of the Founder of our Art, resolve that there be spread upon our records the remembrance not only of the fact that he was the Inventor of the Telephone, but also of the fact that the spirit of service and the devotion to duty which have become characteristic of the system which bears his name were characteristic also of him personally;

And, turning to the future, we resolve, both young and old, that we, in that same spirit, will carry on the work which he began, until all the world are neighbors and all nations friends.

The Presiding officer then turned the attention of the Convention to the history of the telephone art by announcing that there were two addresses to be presented to the meeting. The first of these was by F. P. Lewis about the opening of the first line between Boston and Providence in January, 1881, and of an experimental line through to New York. This was followed by a talk by Walter D. McKinney about times in the old Telephone Despatch Company. These addresses led to a most interesting and delightful exchange in reminiscences in which Mr. Lewis and Mr. McKinney were joined informally by H. J. Pettengill, who in the old times had been with one of the opposition companies, the American Rapid Automatic Telegraph Company, and by General Carty. It was altogether a sort of reunion of the four at which the rest of the Pioneers had the pleasure and privilege of sitting in, a most valuable way of getting much historical material safely recorded.

The session of Friday evening was held in the new Cleveland Public Auditorium. Some 14,000 people were present. E. A. Reed presided. Mayor Kohler was pre-sented and made a brief address, and General Carty ex-pressed to the large Cleveland audience the appreciation of the Pioneers for the welcome they had been accorded in the city. The chief address of the evening was by the Hon. Newton D. Baker, former Mayor of Cleveland and Secre-tary of War in President Wilson's cabinet. After this ad-dress General Carty conducted a Long Lines-Loud Speaker Demonstration including a roll-call of the continent from Cleveland to San Francisco and down over the Key West Telephone Cable to Havana. It closed with the sounding of Taps in San Francisco, which rang through the large Auditorium in Cleveland, and the good-night responses back along the Transcontinental Telephone Line to Cleve-land.

At Cleveland as at all the cities where the Telephone Pioneers had held their Conventions the entertainment began at latest with the arrival of the Pioneers in the city and can hardly be said to have ended with their departure. Hospitality was in the air and expressions of it were con-tinuous. On Saturday, September 30th, the entertainment and hospitality centered at the Cleveland Yacht Club. There luncheon was served and boats were placed at the disposal of the visitors. In the evening the Pioneers gath-ered at the Masonic Temple for the banquet and a review called "Back from '76 to '22." The souvenir was an elabo-rately decorated menu card bearing a portrait of H. B. Thayer, with scenes of his career interwoven into the decorative border and a picture of the statue by Evelyn

Longman, The Spirit of Electricity, which stands on top of the tower of the Telephone Building in New York.

The Committee of Arrangements for the Cleveland Convention consisted of R. H. Starrett and B. A. Kaiser, with a General Committee of which E. A. Reed was Chairman and D. H. Morris, Secretary, and eight other local committees.

* * * * *

By virtue of the vitality of the Telephone Pioneers of America, and by virtue of the fact that the organization exists to be pioneer and to do pioneer work, as well as to record pioneer achievements, this historical account of how it has grown is not complete and cannot be completed. The twelve years of the Telephone Pioneers of America will continue into many more, and this historical sketch of them can only discontinue temporarily, asking leave to print from time to time later on, each time no doubt reviewing the whole story in the new light of the new progress and new achievements of the Pioneer spirit in the Telephone industry and in this its Telephone Pioneer citadel.

But such a bird's-eye view as this, it is hoped, will have practical value by making evident the power of the forces that have been shaping up the organization and the quality of the big things that are being accomplished in the annual meetings. In one way, every one will recognize that the Telephone Pioneers is the same in every way as it was in 1911, when started by Henry W. Pope. Charles R. Truex, and Thomas B. Doolittle, the only changes, whether in purpose or in form, being such as were necessary to keep it the same and to rescue it from the weathering in the

changed conditions to which it has been exposed, especially
since the war. In another way, every one must see that the
Telephone Pioneers is quite different. In size, in strength,
in influence, and therefore in opportunity and function, the
Telephone Pioneers has grown enormously. It began with
but 745 members at the time of the Boston meeting in 1911.
In 1922, at the time of the Cleveland meeting the membership had reached 4,276. And at the time of this writing,
August, 1923, the number has reached 5,625. These figures are not merely measures of membership. They are
typical of the buoyant growth of the Telephone Pioneers
in every respect. In 1911 the organization was born, a
healthly child. Now, in 1923, it is a young man, keen for
a future of great usefulness.

Finally, the purpose of this little book will have been
served if it enables its readers to see in convenient compass,
as through a reducing glass, the fine symmetry and quality of
the Telephone Pioneers. For the significance of the association is to be found in the wholesome solidarity that such
an organization fosters in a corporation or an industry
between the officers and the employes, all alike, on the basis
of continued service and accomplishment together. The
interest of all is the same. The Telephone Pioneers exem-
plifies that splendid fact. For it is full of great promise for
the industrial life of America that in so important an industry as the Telephone all work, through and through and
from top to bottom, is dominated by a real spirit of comradeship.

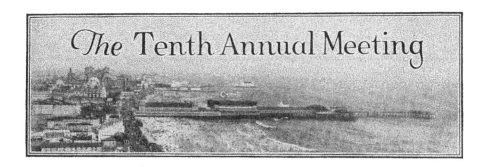

The Tenth Annual Meeting

Atlantic City, N. J., "The Playground of the World," was the scene of the Tenth Annual Meeting of the Telephone Pioneers of America and the Second Meeting of the General Assembly on October 19 and 20, 1923, The Bell Telephone Company of Pennsylvania being the host.

Not even the largest of the city's hotels could house the big assemblage of telephone men and women, so the famous "Million Dollar Pier" was taken over in its entirety by the Pioneers for their meetings. This pier was constructed by Capt. J. L. Young in 1905 at a cost of $1,250,000 and it extends from the Boardwalk out into the ocean for a distance of 1,600 feet.

Probably no other place in this country or in Europe is so much the playground of "The World and His Wife" as is Atlantic City. The crowd to be found along the famous Boardwalk is a most cosmopolitan one. It includes persons of wealth who pay almost fabulous sums for suites in the big hotels, and modest-pursed excursionists whose means permit no more than a narrow room in some boarding house and meals at a lunch counter. But pleas-

The Boardwalk at Steeplechase Pier

The Chelsea

ure is not always computed in dimes and dollars and the humblest vacationist not infrequently will have more real sport than the man whose expenses for himself and family run into hundreds of dollars per week.

Atlantic City stands on Absecon Island which is a long bar of sand separated from the New Jersey mainland by an expanse of bays and salt marshes. It is sixty miles from Philadelphia and one hundred and fifty miles from New York by rail. The first permanent settler on the Island was Jeremiah Leeds who in 1804 built a log hut near what is now the corner of Missouri and Arctic Avenues. Leeds added to his original purchase until he owned the entire island, and in 1816 leased a part of it to John Bryant who was the second settler.

In 1852 a few other settlers had moved in and the feasibility of a railroad connecting the Island to Philadelphia was discussed. Work on

The Ambassa[dor]

The Ritz-Carlton

such a road was begun a few months later and the road was completed July 1, 1854. On July 4 of that year the first excursion train entered the seashore resort, the forerunner of countless thousands of trains that were to come later. This first train was hauled by an old wood-burning engine and the passengers who sat on board seats on open cars were much annoyed by cinders that burned holes in their clothes.

The permanent residents of the city at that time did not exceed one hundred and the "hotel" accommodations consisted principally of Jeremiah Leeds' old boarding house.

The permanent population of Atlantic City today exceeds 52,000 while in mid-summer it houses at least 300,000 residents and visitors. There is a daily fluctuation of about 100,000 around the week ends during July and August and it has been estimated that 500 business men commute daily between Atlantic City and Phila-

The Traymoi

The "Fish Haul" on the Million Dollar Pier

Part of the "Pleasure Fleet" at the Inlet

Garden Pier Theatre Built over the Ocean

Looking Down the Boardwalk Toward "Pioneer Headquarters"

delphia, Trenton, Wilmington, and other inland points during the summer.

This floating population places Atlantic City in a position not held by any other city in the world and it presents some intricate and peculiar problems to the telephone company and other public utilities which must provide for such an unusual "peak load."

In recent years a great effort has been put forth by the permanent population of Atlantic City to establish it as an all-year-'round resort.

Atlantic City was the inventor of the Boardwalk, since copied so widely by other seaside resorts. The first Boardwalk was completed in 1870 at a cost of $4500 and was about 16 feet wide and nearly three miles long. This original promenade has been rebuilt and extended many times until today the Boardwalk is eight miles long and is sixty feet wide for a great part of its length, being the longest

and finest construction of its kind in the world, although it has been copied widely.

Several fine automobile highways lead into the city, the principal one being the White Horse Pike between Atlantic City and Camden, motorists being ferried from the latter point to Philadelphia across the Delaware River.

With the completion of the Bridge across the Delaware River at Philadelphia in 1926 it is expected that increased motor traffic will make a second highway between that point and Atlantic City necessary.

Entrance to the Million Dollar Pier

Telephone Pioneers of America

NATIONAL OFFICERS AND EXECUTIVE COMMITTEE FOR 1923

President
LEONARD H. KINNARD

Past President
JOHN J. CARTY

Senior Vice President
F. A. STEVENSON

Vice Presidents

JAMES T. MORAN   J. A. STEWART
E. A. REED

Secretary   *Treasurer*
R. H. STARRETT   F. A. BUTTRICK
195 Broadway, New York City   .

Executive Committee
One Year Term

B. A. KAISER   J. E. WARREN

Two Years' Term
VERNE RAY   MARY MILLER
E. K. HALL

Telephone Pioneers of America

CHAPTER ORGANIZATIONS
AS OF OCTOBER 1, 1923

❧

THEODORE N. VAIL CHAPTER No. 1
212 West Washington Street, Chicago, Ill.

OFFICERS

President	Jerome D. Kennedy
Vice President	William E. Bell
Secretary-Treasurer	W. J. Maiden

EXECUTIVE COMMITTEE

John P. Hansen   Miss S. Cornelia Young

❧

N. C. KINGSBURY CHAPTER No. 2
4300 Euclid Avenue, Cleveland, O.

OFFICERS

President	E. A. Reed
Vice President	C. P. Bradford
Vice President	A. J. Mellen
Vice President	A. B. Wood
Vice President	W. S. Hays
Secretary	Norman Anderson
Treasurer	E. J. Farrell

EXECUTIVE COMMITTEE

E. A. Reed   C. P. Bradford
A. J. Mellen   A. B. Wood
W. S. Hays

KILGOUR CHAPTER No. 3
225 East Fourth Street, Cincinnati, Ohio

OFFICERS

President	B. L. Kilgour
Vice President	R. C. Hall
Secretary	W. G. Betty
Treasurer	Miss Millie Landman

EXECUTIVE COMMITTEE
N. E. Westlake   James Harper

W. Frank Armstrong

ಞ

WISCONSIN CHAPTER No. 4
418 Broadway, Milwaukee, Wis.

OFFICERS

President	Leslie Killam
Vice President	F. M. McEniry
Secretary	Franklyn J. Mayer
Treasurer	W. W. Hiller

EXECUTIVE COMMITTEE
James T. Quinlan   Phillip J. Skolsky

William N. Cash   Mrs. Ella Markey

Miss Marie Mentink

ಞ

EMPIRE CHAPTER No. 5
15 Dey Street, New York, N. Y.

OFFICERS

President	Burch Foraker
Vice President	C. A. Spaulding
Secretary	H. J. Schultz
Treasurer	E. A. Gurnee

EXECUTIVE COMMITTEE
Miss K. M. Schmitt   F. H. Leggett

J. F. X. O'Hea

LIBERTY BELL CHAPTER No. 6
⸱ 1631 Arch Street, Philadelphia, Pa.

OFFICERS

President   C. A. Janke
Vice President   F. I. Daly
Secretary   A. Bunton
Treasurer   Miss Mary Miller

EXECUTIVE COMMITTEE

J. Cunningham   Miss M. I. White
Miss Katherine S. Spielberger

❦

CENTRAL PENNSYLVANIA CHAPTER No. 7
19 South Second Street, Harrisburg, Pa.

OFFICERS

President   C. B. Smith
Vice President   H. F. Hope
Secretary   Miss Mary E. Beatty
Treasurer   Miss Imogene I. Malaney

EXECUTIVE COMMITTEE

Chairman, Thos. McKeon
Miss Minnie E. Hennigh   Miss Grace Keller
D. I. Swenk   H. P. Troxell

❦

ROCKY MOUNTAIN CHAPTER No. 8
1421 Champa Street, Denver, Colo

OFFICERS

President   A. S. Peters
Vice President   C. A. Wiswell
Secretary   H. W. Bellard
Treasurer   ————————

EXECUTIVE COMMITTEE

Chairman, Waldo Cockrell
H. W. Kline   C. E. Stratton

MORRIS F. TYLER CHAPTER No. 9
157 Church Street, New Haven, Conn.

OFFICERS

President	James T. Moran
Secretary	F. P. Lewis
Treasurer	C. B. Doolittle

ੴ

WOLVERINE CHAPTER No. 10
1365 Cass Avenue, Detroit, Mich.

OFFICERS

President	George P. Holland
Vice President	Miss Estelle McGraw
Secretary	H. E. Harrington
Treasurer	William L. Burrows

EXECUTIVE COMMITTEE

W. J. Berry	Miss Estelle McGraw
George P. Holland	William L. Burrows
C. Kittredge	H. E. Harrington

ੴ

GEORGE F. DURANT CHAPTER No. 11
314 North Broadway, St. Louis, Mo.

OFFICERS

President	J. K. Wass
Vice President	R. M. Moss
Secretary	F. Woltage
Treasurer	Miss Clara Linens

H. G. McCULLY CHAPTER No. 12
309 Washington Street, Newark, N. J.

OFFICERS

President	John F. Murphy
Vice President	Miss Minnie A. Jones
Vice President	Daniel J. Sullivan
Vice President	Eugene C. Estep
Secretary	Henry G. Eaton
Treasurer	C. Walter Van Zee

EXECUTIVE COMMITTEE

John F. Naylon   Miss Dora E. Ulrich
George H. Merrill   William C. Graham
Andrew J. Donohue

✝

WESTERN PENNSYLVANIA CHAPTER No. 13
416 Seventh Avenue, Pittsburgh, Pa.

OFFICERS

President	J. A. Magerry
Vice President	Miss Mary F. Jackson
Secretary	J. Howard Moore
Treasurer	Edgar Henderson

EXECUTIVE COMMITTEE

J. A. Magerry   C. A. Beam
M. J. Bishop   Z. C. Gillespie
Edgar Henderson   Miss Mary F. Jackson
J. Howard Moore

✝

THOMAS SHERWIN CHAPTER No. 14
50 Oliver Street, Boston, Mass.

OFFICERS

President	Edwin M. Surprise
Vice President	Henry McDonald
Secretary-Treasurer	F. J. Boynton

The above officers constitute the Executive Committee.

ALEXANDER GRAHAM BELL CHAPTER No. 15
725 Thirteenth Street, N. W., Washington, D. C.

OFFICERS

President	Burdett Stryker
Vice President	G. H. Warren
Vice President	R. L. Wright
Vice President	G. W. Thrall
Secretary-Treasurer	Miss Carolyn H. Martin

EXECUTIVE COMMITTEE

Harry Ellis	Miss Emma J. Grady
J. L. Harrington	Fred D. Petty

ಆ

HOOSIER STATE CHAPTER No. 16
C/o Indiana Bell Telephone Co., Indianapolis, Ind.

OFFICERS

President	E. L. Hamlin
Sr. Vice President	E. T. Bonds
Vice President	J. L. Wayne, III
Secretary	Miss Margaret Cooper
Treasurer	A. R. Henry

EXECUTIVE COMMITTEE

E. L. Hamlin	E. T. Bonds
J. L. Wayne, III	C. S. Norton
J. E. Carver	

ಆ

HAWKEYE CHAPTER No. 17
C/o Northwestern Bell Telephone Co., Des Moines, Iowa

OFFICERS

President	H. G. Conger
Vice President	F. D. Cleaver
Secretary-Treasurer	Miss Julia I. Dwyer

C. P. WAINMAN CHAPTER No. 18

C/o Northwestern Bell Telephone Co., Minneapolis, Minn.

OFFICERS

President	George A. French
Vice President	E. C. Short
Secretary-Treasurer	Ross Wheeler

❦

CASPER E. YOST CHAPTER No. 19

118 South 19th Street, Omaha, Neb.

OFFICERS

President	Charles E. Hall
Vice President	A. A. Lowman
Secretary-Treasurer	W. W. Davenport

❦

WILLIAM J. DENVER CHAPTER No. 20

295 Worthington Street, Springfield, Mass.

OFFICERS

President	S. F. Parker
Vice President	Frank C. Buck
Secretary-Treasurer	T. F. Maguire

The above officers constitute the Executive Committee.

❦

TENNESSEE CHAPTER No. 21

Third Avenue and Church Street, Nashville, Tenn.

OFFICERS

President	Leland Hume
Vice President	James N. Cox
Vice President	A. T. McNelley
Vice President	Mrs. W. H. Brower
Vice President	Estes Young
Treasurer	Foster Hume
Secretary	Kendrick C. Hardcastle

EXECUTIVE COMMITTEE

J. H. Baker	W. K. Boardman
W. T. Edwards	Frank Flournoy

E. F. Garratt

LONE STAR CHAPTER No. 22
Western Indemnity. Building, Dallas, Tex.

OFFICERS
President   J. E. Farnsworth
Vice President   J. F. Henderson
Secretary   W. A. Biggs
Treasurer   W. R. Faught

The above officers constitute the Executive Committee.

℞

DIXIE CHAPTER No. 23
78 South Pryor Street, Atlanta, Ga.

OFFICERS
President   F. E. Montague
Sr. Vice President   W. H. Adkins
Vice President   W. H. M. Weaver
Vice President   J. Smith Lanier
Vice President   W. T. Gentry
Secretary   W. G. Rauch
Treasurer   J. W. Gibson

EXECUTIVE COMMITTEE
M. B. Speir   W. B. Wallace
F. E. Montague   Miss Sammie Dickson
J. E. Warren   W. H. Adkins

℞

GULF CHAPTER No. 24
C/o Cumberland Tel. & Tel. Co., New Orleans, La.

OFFICERS
President   C. A. Stair
Vice President   R. Dean
Vice President   J. C. Rourke, Sr.
Vice President   E. W. Gibbons
Vice President   D. W. Lacy
Secretary-Treasurer W. T. Naff

EXECUTIVE COMMITTEE
J. S. Gillentine   Mrs. E. F. Shannon
Rene Gonzales   C. E. Forshey
R. H. Mullen

EDWARD J. HALL CHAPTER No. 25

195 Broadway, New York, N. Y.

OFFICERS

President   A. L. Salt
Vice President   C. H. Hadlock
Secretary-Treasurer   H. E. Willard

❦

CHARLES FLEETFORD SISE CHAPTER No. 26

C/o The Bell Telephone Co. of Canada, Montreal, P. Q.

OFFICERS

President   L. B. McFarlane
Vice President   K. J. Dunstan
Secretary-Treasurer   W. H. Black

EXECUTIVE COMMITTEE

L. B. McFarlane   K. J. Dunstan
W. H. Black   O. E. Stanton
A. G. Watson

CPSIA information can be obtained
at www.ICGtesting.com
Printed in the USA
BVHW041413180119
538187BV00015B/742/P